Verses From
The West Country

Edited by Lynsey Hawkins

Young Writers

First published in Great Britain in 2007 by:
Young Writers
Remus House
Coltsfoot Drive
Peterborough
PE2 9JX
Telephone: 01733 890066
Website: www.youngwriters.co.uk

SB ISBN 978-1 84602 938 7

Foreword

Young Writers was established in 1991 and has been passionately devoted to the promotion of reading and writing in children and young adults ever since. The quest continues today. Young Writers remains as committed to the nurturing of poetic and literary talent as ever.

This year's Young Writers competition has proven as vibrant and dynamic as ever and we are delighted to present a showcase of the best poetry from across the UK and in some cases overseas. Each poem has been selected from a wealth of *Little Laureates* entries before ultimately being published in this, our sixteenth primary school poetry series.

Once again, we have been supremely impressed by the overall quality of the entries we have received. The imagination, energy and creativity which has gone into each young writer's entry made choosing the poems a challenging and often difficult but ultimately hugely rewarding task - the general high standard of the work submitted ensured this opportunity to bring their poetry to a larger appreciative audience.

We sincerely hope you are pleased with this final collection and that you will enjoy *Little Laureates Verses From The West Country* for many years to come.

Contents

Farrington Gurney CE Primary School, Farrington Gurney

Amy Harmer (8)	33
Rebecca Thompson (8)	34
Mary Appleton (9)	35
Darcy Short (10)	36
Alice Vosper (11)	37
Amy Turner (11)	38
Daniel Watts (10)	39
Emily Bannister (10)	40
Karah Smith (9)	41
Callum Davis (11)	42
Bethany Ives (9)	43
Paige Matthews (11)	44

Monteclefe CE (VA) Junior School, Somerton

Connor Matts (10)	45
Kieran Richards (9)	46
Alicia Harvey (10)	47
Ashleigh Edwards (10)	48
Lucy Bond (10)	49
Chloë Fisher (9)	50
Emily Brown (11)	51
Olivia Stone (10)	52
Elina Dyer (10)	53
Cadence Lark (10)	54
Tyler Higgs (9)	55
Megan Lacey (10)	56
Emma Daley (11)	57
Gemma Blayney (10)	58
Patrick Bromley (9)	59
Josie Mitchell (10)	60
Bonnie White (10)	61
Joshua Bennett (9)	62
Megan Bradley (11)	63
Georgia Raybould (10)	64
Charlie Sillence (10)	65
Rebecca Irving (10)	66
Ryan Wheadon (10)	67
Lauren Cattle (9)	68
Amelia Lowe (10)	69

St Michael's Junior School, Bath

Sophie Waldron (8)	70
Liam Herron (8)	71
Trey Harding (8)	72
Declan Tonkinson (9)	73
Bradley Blackmore (8)	74

Silverhill School, Bristol

Toby Ashman (9)	75
Louis Johnson (9)	76
Rosaleen Farrell (8)	77
Anna-Louise Morgan (9)	78
Olivia Stewart (11)	79
Jamie Stephens (10)	80
Chelsie Sparks (10)	81
Katie Farrell (11)	82
Sam Bird (10)	83
Ellie Seal (9)	84
Huw Tingley (9)	85
Harry Collins (10)	86
Toby Champion (10)	87
Stephanie Thorndyke (10)	88
Emma Robinson (10)	89
Tvesha Parikh (9)	90
Evelyn Gardner (10)	91
Ayesha Bedi (10)	92
Joshua Tucker (10)	93
Emma Portno (7)	94
Eugene Tebbenham-Small (8)	95
Samuel Thorndyke (8)	96
Emma Ujvari (8)	97
Madison Dawson (7)	98
Neha Mehta (8)	99
Izzy Tippins (7)	100
Sophie Walker (7)	101
Jacob Evans (8)	102
Christian Smith (9)	103
Lauren Childs (8)	104
Lewis Griffiths (8)	105
Ellie-Mae Dodd (8)	106
Annalise Jones (8)	107

The Poems

Fireworks

Fire burning brightly
Shadows creeping cautiously
Rockets banging noisily
Giving everyone a fright

Children watching excitedly
While the fire burns beautifully
Coloured fireworks blasting off
Into the sparkly, starry sky

Sparklers twinkle prettily
Guy Fawkes burning quickly
Catherine wheels spinning round and round
While sparks fall to the ground.

Aerin Phillips (9)
Berrow CE Primary School, Burnham on Sea

Dad, Can You Rap?

(Inspired by 'Gran, Can You Rap?' by Jack Ouseby)

Dad was in his chair,
He was taking a snooze,
He was snoring like a bear,
Listening to the news,
He's the best rapping dad this world's ever seen,
He's a tip-top, drip-drop, rap-rap king.

When I tapped him on the shoulder,
To see if he could rap,
'Dad can you rap? Can you, Dad?'
He opened one eye and said to me,
'Man, I'm the best rapping dad this world's ever seen,
I'm a slip-slop, yip-yap, rap-rap king.'

Then he started to jump,
Then wow with a bump,
This way and that,
He looked really cool,
In a nice big hat,
He's the best rapping dad this world's ever seen,
He's a nip-nap, bip-bop, rap-rap king.

Sarah Wall (9)
Berrow CE Primary School, Burnham on Sea

Gran, Can You Rap?

(Inspired by 'Gran, Can You Rap?' by Jack Ouseby)

She rapped down the stairs and through the door,
She rapped halfway out and shouted, 'Goals galore.'
She rapped past me and then Theirry Henry,
She rapped past Theirry and shouted, 'Pompey.'
She's the best rapping gran this world's ever seen,
She's a nip-nap, yip-yap, rap-rap queen.

She rapped to the shop and bought a lollipop,
She stole a drink and got caught by a cop,
She was rapping in court and got five days,
She was dreaming about large stingrays.
She's the best rapping gran this world's ever seen,
She's a tip-top, flip-flop, rap-rap queen.

Oliver Morris & Ashley Harper (8)
Berrow CE Primary School, Burnham on Sea

Gran, Can You Rap?

(Inspired by 'Gran, Can You Rap?' by Jack Ouseby)

She rapped upstairs and she rapped in the room
She ran downstairs with a bim-bam-boom
She rapped past me and she rapped past you
She rapped so hard that she lost her shoe
She's the best rapping gran this world's ever seen
She's a tip-top, hip-hop, rap-rap queen.

She rapped past the dog and she rapped past the cat
She rapped in her coat and she rapped in her hat
She rapped on the fence and she rapped on the door
She rapped on the chair and she rapped some more
She's the best rapping gran this world's ever seen
She's a yip-yap, slip-slap, rap-rap queen.

She rapped past the shops and got some bananas
She looked in the mirror and saw her pyjamas
She rapped past the market and tapped her feet
As she rapped, she danced to the beat
She's the best rapping gran this world's ever seen
She's a hip-hap, lip-lap, rap-rap queen.

**Yanika Johnson (7), Chloe Parish, Dominic Nagiel,
Harvey Nagiel, Nesta Patrick, Sarah Fiddes (8) &
Rhiannon Fletcher (9)**
Berrow CE Primary School, Burnham on Sea

Gran, Can You Rap?

(Inspired by 'Gran, Can You Rap?' by Jack Ouseby)

Gran was in her chair, she was taking a nap,
When I tapped her on the shoulder to see if she could rap.
'Gran, can you rap? Can you rap? Can you, Gran?'
And she opened one eye and she said to me,
'Man, I'm the best rapping gran this world's ever seen,
I'm a tip-top, slip-slop, rap-rap queen.'

She rapped past my cat and she rapped past my dog,
She rapped up and down like a little baby frog.
She bounced up and down like a grown up Tigger,
She rapped down the road and rapped in a digger.
She's the best rapping gran this world's ever seen,
She's a clip-clop, flick-flock, rap-rap queen.

And she rose from the digger in the middle of the road,
And she rapped in the river as it flowed.
She rapped through a field and she rapped by the cows,
She rapped with her friend, Mrs Plows.
She's the best rapping gran this world's ever seen,
She's a bim-bam, tim-tam, rap-rap queen.

She rapped out the field and she rapped in the town,
She rapped in the shop and she bought a big crown.
She rapped out the shop and she rapped down the street,
The neighbours all cheered as they tapped their feet.
She's the best rapping gran this world's ever seen,
She's a rick-rock, brick-brock, rap-rap queen.

She rapped back home and she rapped to the table,
She rapped past me and my dog, Mabel.
She rapped upstairs and she fell back down,
She bumped her head and made a frown.

Ashley Stearn & Lily Horwood (9), Alex Dermanis (8)
Berrow CE Primary School, Burnham on Sea

Gran, Can You Rap?

(Based on 'Gran, Can You Rap?' by Jack Ouseby)

She rapped in her bedroom and fell on her bed,
She tried doing a handstand but she landed on her head.
She rapped in the kitchen and the pots went *clang,*
She tumbled over with a great big *bang.*
She's the best rapping gran this world's ever seen,
She's a hip-hop, nip-nop, rap-rap queen.

Gemma Smith (9)
Berrow CE Primary School, Burnham on Sea

Gran, Can You Rap?

(Based on 'Gran, Can You Rap?' by Jack Ouseby)

Gran was in her chair, she was taking a nap,
When I tapped her on the shoulder to see if she could rap.
'Gran, can you rap? Can you rap? Can you, Gran?'
And she opened one eye and she said to me,
'Man, I'm the best rapping gran this world's ever seen,
I'm a tip-top, hip-hop, rap-rap queen.'

She rapped past my dog and she rapped past my cat,
Whilst a little baby hamster was sitting in her hat.
She sat on the sofa which was made of black leather,
She couldn't go outside, it was very bad weather.
She's the best rapping gran this world's ever seen,
She's a tip-top, slip-stop, rap-rap queen.

She saw a busy bee just sitting on her knee,
When she was on holiday getting in the sea.
She was coming back from holiday, so she said bye-bye,
She got on the plane and went up in the sky.
She's the best rapping gran this world's ever seen,
She's a clip-clop, hip-hop, rap-rap queen.

Aerin Phillips & Emma McCarthy (9)
Berrow CE Primary School, Burnham on Sea

Gran, Can You Rap?

(Based on 'Gran, Can You Rap?' by Jack Ouseby)

She rapped in the kitchen and stepped on a pin,
When she wasn't looking, she fell in the bin.
Then she rapped up the stairs and into her room,
And she stamped to the bed with a bam, bam, boom.
'I'm the best rapping gran this world's ever seen,
I'm a zip-zap, click-clack, rap-rap queen.'

She rapped past the street and rapped by the poor,
But there on the floor was an apple core.
She rapped in a plane way up high,
When she was rapping, she told a lie.
'I'm the best rapping gran this world's ever seen,
I'm a plip-plop, rick-rock, rap-rap queen.'

Georgia Tonkin (8)
Berrow CE Primary School, Burnham on Sea

Gran, Can You Rap?

(Based on 'Gran, Can You Rap?' by Jack Ouseby)

She rapped up the stairs and she rapped in the room,
She ran down the stairs with a bim, bam, boom.
She rapped past me and she rapped past you,
She rapped so hard that she lost her shoe.
She's the best rapping gran this world's ever seen,
She's a tip-top, hip-hop, rap-rap queen.

She rapped under the table and she rapped through the door,
She rapped down the street past the rich and the poor.
She rapped in the cloakroom, she rapped in the cupboard,
She rapped in the freezer and she shivered and shuddered.
She's the best rapping gran this world's ever seen,
She's a tick-tock, chip-chop, rap-rap queen.

She rapped past the radio going la-la-la,
She rapped past me and she passed my old granpa.
She rapped past the mouse asking for some cheese,
She really wanted some, so she begged, please, please.
She's the best rapping gran this world's ever seen,
She's a crip-crop, ship-shop, rap-rap queen.

She rapped on the chair going whizz, whizz, whizz,
She crashed into the wall and got full of dizz.
She rapped in the corridor and she was looking at the work
And there was a picture of a parrot going peck-peck-peck.
She's the best rapping gran this world's ever seen,
She's a pish-posh, crish-crosh, rap-rap queen.

Corey Hayward, Sarah Fiddes, Robert Anderson (8)
& James Maddern (7)
Berrow CE Primary School, Burnham on Sea

Gran, Can You Rap?

(Based on 'Gran, Can You Rap?' by Jack Ouseby)

She rapped down the lane in agony and pain,
She rapped to the hospital and it started to rain.
She went inside, rapping still,
Then the nurse told her to take a pill.
After a while she was at the tills,
Paying and shopping for all the bills.
She's the best rapping gran this world's ever seen,
She's a bip-bop, hip-hop, rap-rap queen.

She rapped up the stairs and rapped in the room,
She ran down the stairs with a bim, bam, boom.
She rapped past me and Theirry Henry,
She's the best rapping gran this world's ever seen,
She's a pip-pop, chip-chop, rap-rap queen.

William Garland & Jack Goodall (8)
Berrow CE Primary School, Burnham on Sea

My Rapping Gran

(Based on 'Gran, Can You Rap?' by Jack Ouseby)

She rapped up the stairs and in the room
She rapped on her bed with a bim, bam, boom.
She's the best rapping gran this world's ever seen,
She's a tip-top, hip-hop, rap-rap queen.

I've got a gran and her name is Fay
She rapped in her sleep and she rapped all day.
She rapped in her work and she rapped at play
She 'wraps' my presents for my birthday.
She's the best rapping gran this world's ever seen,
She's a flip-flop, hip-hop, rap-rap queen.

Dominic Nagiel (8)
Berrow CE Primary School, Burnham on Sea

Gran, Can You Rap?

(Based on 'Gran, Can You Rap?' by Jack Ouseby)

She rapped in America, she rapped in Spain,
And she came home rapping on an aeroplane.
She rapped on the telly, it was really cool,
When she came back home we were having a ball.
'I'm the best rapping gran this world's ever seen,
I'm a slip-slop, flip-flop, rap-rap queen.'

The next day she woke up, she was really shattered,
She fell down the stairs, banged and clattered.
She went out shopping to get some food
And she came home in a very grumpy mood.
She's the best rapping gran this world's ever seen,
She's a bish-bash, smish-smash, rap-rap queen.

The next day she left, she was really sad,
Her grandchildren said, 'It's not that bad.'
She said, 'Give me time, I need to recover.'
She sobbed in pain and said to my mother,
'I'm the best rapping gran this world's ever seen,
I'm a tip-top, snip-snap, rap-rap queen.'

Sophie Bessell (9) & Megan Masters (7)
Berrow CE Primary School, Burnham on Sea

Gran, Can You Rap?

(Based on 'Gran, Can You Rap?' by Jack Ouseby)

Gran was in her deckchair taking a nap,
When I whispered in her ear, 'Hey Gran, can you rap?'
Then she jumped up quick and lifted me high,
And she said to me, 'I can rap till I die!'

She's the best rapping gran this world's ever seen,
She's a yip-yap, tip-tap, rap-rap queen.

She rapped past me and she rapped past you,
She rapped so hard that she fell down the loo!
She rapped in the garden and she rapped in the shed,
As she was rapping, this is what she said:

'I'm the best rapping gran this world's ever seen,
I'm a wip-wap, slip-slap, rap-rap queen.'

Ben Ayers (9) & Samuel Yard (8)
Berrow CE Primary School, Burnham on Sea

Gran, Can You Rap?

(Based on 'Gran, Can You Rap?' by Jack Ouseby)

She rapped when she walked and she rapped when she flew,
She rapped in the sea and caught the flu.
She rapped past me and she rapped past a tin,
She rapped so hard that she landed in a bin.
She's the best rapping gran this world's ever seen,
She's a flip-flop, clip-clop, rap-rap queen.

William Lupton (9)
Berrow CE Primary School, Burnham on Sea

Gran, Can You Rap?

(Based on 'Gran, Can You Rap?' by Jack Ouseby)

She rapped around the world,
She rapped up a hill,
She rapped to the shop,
She is rapping still.
She's the best rapping gran this world's ever seen,
She's a hip-hop, trip-trop, rap-rap queen.

She's the best rapping gran you could ever hope to see,
She hips and hops everywhere she goes
And I'm glad she's related to me.
She's the best rapping gran this world's ever seen,
She's a trip-trap, clip-clap, rap-rap queen.

Emmy Dymond (7)
Berrow CE Primary School, Burnham on Sea

Arsenal

Henry, Van Persie and the team,
Go forward to win every trophy they see.
The Premier League, the FA Cup, The Champions League,
The Carling Cup,
They're all for one and one for all,
They beat Man Utd, six goals to four.

In the Carling Cup but who?
Arsenal of course, that's true.
Beat Liverpool 6-3 in the Carling Cup,
Then beat them again in the FA Cup.

Gunners their nickname, what a team,
They'll win every trophy, you'll see.
Highbury was their last ground,
Then the Emirates they found.

Henry, Van Persie and the team,
Will win every trophy,
Just wait and see.

Matthew Derham (11)
Blackbrook Primary School, Taunton

The Stormy Seashore

Crashing waves like galloping horses,
Water flying onto the dirty docks.

Waves making the boats bob up and down,
Seagulls nipping at people's chips.

Sand flying, blinding my eyes,
Pebbles being thrown in the sea.

Belinda Thompson (11)
Blackbrook Primary School, Taunton

Superheroes

I wish I could be like you,
Ninjas, Batman, Superman too.
Cowboy Spiderman, he's the best,
He has laser beams on his chest.
But he has an enemy, Lazer Carrot,
He has a sidekick, Barry the Parrot.
But there's one more man, he's lord of the sea,
Guess what! It's me!

Tom Cherrie (10)
Blackbrook Primary School, Taunton

An Australian Summer's Day

An Australian summer's day,
Fifty kangaroos jump and play,
And koalas frolic and squeak,
A summer Christmas I seek.

On a golden, sandy beach,
When holidaymakers fold their sheets,
The sand blinding my eyes
And then seagulls fly in the sky.

Samuel Wooler (10)
Blackbrook Primary School, Taunton

A Theme Park

Candyfloss, candyfloss, hurry,
Doughnuts, doughnuts, lovely and sweet,
Chocolate, chocolate, scrummy,
Hot dogs, hot dogs, lovely and hot.

See children eating sweets,
See children running place to place,
See children rolling in fun houses,
See children walking in.

Feel the butterflies in your tummy as you go,
Feel scared when you go upside down,
Feel sad when you leave.

Hear adults shouting time to go,
Hear adults screaming at their kids,
Hear children crying when they're hurt.

Thomas Richards (11)
Blackbrook Primary School, Taunton

Playing With My Brothers

Playing with Charlie and Jack can be fun,
Playing with toys is boring, but at least they like it.
Their favourite game is hide-and-seek,
Probably because they win so much.
Charlie makes it really hard though,
Because he says, '1, 80, ready or not, here I come!'
By the time they get bored,
They have literally destroyed the house!

Kieran Palmer (10)
Blackbrook Primary School, Taunton

The Seashore At Night

Gigantic waves making a lonely figure,
Through the lonely, silent night.
Pebbles crashing on the shore
And fish stuck in nets.

The fishermen swishing their nets,
Fish swimming in the lonely night.
The fishermen coming back,
Leaving a trail of water behind them.

Sarah Hollebon (10)
Blackbrook Primary School, Taunton

The Landing

Something very special happened one day,
Strange aliens from Zog came to play.
They had three eyes, their bodies were green,
Then I thought it really set a scene.
They walked strangely, they seemed to prance,
Then I noticed they had multicoloured pants.
They liked to play ball, they thought it was the best,
They said it was better than the rest.
They said they had to go,
They wanted to go to a show.
Straight to the saucer they went,
I thought the hull looked rather bent.
They flew in the air, the exhaust was green,
It was the best sight I have ever seen.

Thomas Roach (10)
Blackbrook Primary School, Taunton

At The Seaside

At the seaside where I play football all day.
At the seaside when I go bodyboarding,
I go crashing through the waves.
At the seaside, the bit I like is
Catching crabs until it's night.

Ben Martin (10)
Blackbrook Primary School, Taunton

The Creatures Of The World

In Antarctica the penguins are tottering,
A bear under a beehive likes to do his snoring,
The king of the jungle roaring like mad,
The monkeys can't find anymore bananas, so they're sad.
All types of birds singing,
The tigers' ears are ringing.
All creatures live in a different place,
But now the hare and the tortoise have got to finish their race.

Rhys Cole (10)
Blackbrook Primary School, Taunton

Where Would You Like To Be?

Where would you like to be?
In a park with leaves crunching on the ground,
Children running round and round?
Or in a country where snowballs are melting in the sun,
Children having lots of fun?
Or in spring when flowers start to sprout,
Animals start to pop their heads out?
Or on a seashore where pebbles land in the sea?
Where would you like to be?

Ryan Potter (10)
Blackbrook Primary School, Taunton

The Stormy Jamaican Beach

Dancing trees, dancing trees
Listening to the drum sounds floating on the breeze.

Swirling sand, swirling sand
Crashing into the big, bad sea.

Falling rocks, falling rocks
Falling onto the big, dirty docks.

Crashing waves, crashing waves,
Making the boats ride up and down.

James Smith (10)
Blackbrook Primary School, Taunton

Jeff Hardy

The Intercontinental Champion I see,
Jeff Hardy is the best for me.
The Swanton Bomb, the Twist of Fate,
Oh my God, I cannot wait.

The moonsault, the leg drop
And the entrance too,
And here comes his brother,
With one shoe!

George Lucas (10)
Blackbrook Primary School, Taunton

A Winter's Day

It was the time of winter,
Children playing in the snow,
Making snowmen and throwing snowballs,
Icy windows that needed defrosting,
Icy cars that can't get started up!

The icicles hanging from the gutter, lonely,
Children excitedly putting on their hats, gloves and scarves,
The mist and fog will make you cold,
So please put on your hat and scarf.
Children cannot wait for the white Christmas.
Penguins happily bopping in and out of water.
Are you happy in the winter?

Chloe Bown (10)
Blackbrook Primary School, Taunton

Steam Clouds

She came over she did,
Right up close,
Steam clouds rising
From her nose and her mouth
Big eyes gleaming, sparkly and bright
But not as dark as a winter's midnight.

She came over, she did
Right up close,
I liked her, I did
I liked her the most
Pawing the ground with apparent ease,
Both together in the midsummer's breeze.

Me and my foal
In all weather,
Me and Filly, always together.

Danielle Strickland (11)
Blackbrook Primary School, Taunton

At The Seaside

At the seaside I like to play,
Play with the sand all through the day.

At the seaside, I do go,
Fishing where the rod goes low.

At the seaside, I take my spade,
I also take my bucket and play while I lay.

At the seaside, I like the most,
Whilst lying on the beach I eat toast.

Meg Kirkham (10)
Blackbrook Primary School, Taunton

The Seasons

The season summer
Is beautiful because you can see
The spectacular, gleaming, shining sun
In the middle of the baby-blue, clear sky
Also with the flowers shooting up from the ground.

The season winter
Is amazing because you can see
The gleaming, glistening snow
On top of the long, green grass
In the middle of the fields
With frozen ponds in people's gardens.

The season autumn
Is spectacular because
Of the colour of the leaves.
They are red, brown, yellow and black
You can hear children chasing through them.

The season spring
Is awesome because you can see
The dark yellow daffodils growing
Beside the deep, wavy stream.
Also all the baby animals
Coming into the world.

What wonderful seasons.

Summer Sturmey (11)
Blackbrook Primary School, Taunton

In The Night-Time Sky

In the night-time sky, the ghosts whistle wild.
In the night-time sky, the flowers blow all the while.
In the night-time sky, thunder and lightning strikes.
In the night-time sky, the stars shine bright.
In the night-time sky, the trees swing around.
Under the night-time sky, we are all cosy and warm,
Ready for a scary bedtime storm.

Amy Harmer (8)
Farrington Gurney CE Primary School, Farrington Gurney

Do Not Stand At My Grave And Weep

(Based on 'Do Not Stand At My Grave And Weep' by Mary Frye)

Do not stand at my grave and weep,
As the city of the dead in their graves sleep.
For I am the wind that howls past the moon,
The sky you look up at, I am always there too.

Do not stand at my grave and lean
Over me, because I am happier than I have ever been.
I am the sweet sound of a thrush,
Also I hear no uplifting hush.

Do not stand at my grave and weep,
Please don't remember me when I am gone away.

'Do not stand at my grave and cry,
for I am not there, I did not die.'

Rebecca Thompson (8)
Farrington Gurney CE Primary School, Farrington Gurney

Clouds Travel

Clouds travel near and far,
Sometimes as swiftly as a car,
Sometimes as slowly as a snail,
Clouds can be very pale.

If I were a cloud I'd go anywhere,
Watching people as they stare,
Just floating around in the sky all day,
I'd just want to stay
And never go away . . .

I dream and dream and shout out loud,
I'd love to be a fluffy white cloud,
A cloud that looks like tasty cream,
Wouldn't that be a wonderful dream?

Mary Appleton (9)
Farrington Gurney CE Primary School, Farrington Gurney

Daytime

The sun comes out,
Birds start flying,
Flowers start growing,
Time moves on.

The sun goes down,
The moon comes out,
Stars start to shine,
Time moves on.

The moon fades away,
Daytime returns,
Another day begins,
Time moves on.

Darcy Short (10)
Farrington Gurney CE Primary School, Farrington Gurney

Why?

Why, oh why do the trees sway?
Why, oh why do the squirrels play?
Why, oh why do the birds sing,
Among the flowers of the opening spring?
Why, oh why do the rivers flow?
Why, oh why do the children grow?
Why, oh why do the birds sing,
Among the flowers of the opening spring?
Why, oh why is the sky so blue?
Why, oh why is this season so good?
Why, oh why do the birds sing,
Among the flowers of the opening spring?

Alice Vosper (11)
Farrington Gurney CE Primary School, Farrington Gurney

Little White Rose

Oh, little white rose,
Why do you stand alone?
Oh, little white rose,
Why do you stand and pose?
Oh, little white rose,
Why do you get sprinkled by the hose?
Oh, little white rose,
Why do you have no toes?
Oh, little white rose,
You give joy to my nose.
Oh, little white rose,
You're just yourself, I suppose.

Amy Turner (11)
Farrington Gurney CE Primary School, Farrington Gurney

Birds

Birds
Fly with
Huge, feathery
Wings.
Past towers
And houses
Beaches and farms.
They chirp, sing
And fly. They swoop down when you
Throw bread. They nest in summer trees.
They fly south for
The winter.
They like
To eat
Worms. Birds
Birds, birds,
Birds.

Daniel Watts (10)
Farrington Gurney CE Primary School, Farrington Gurney

Cheetah

Pounce for prey,
Bounce hooray,
Running fast,
Whizzing past,
Zebras fright,
We hunt at night,
Patterned spots,
Little dots,
Pointy ears,
Have no fears,
Long grass,
Sways past,
Hot sun,
Burns my tum.

Emily Bannister (10)
Farrington Gurney CE Primary School, Farrington Gurney

Sadness

Sadness is a . . .

Cold spiky feeling inside of you,
It is just waiting to come out,
So you can be happy too

When you get old you are happy,
Because you're taking another step to Heaven,
But soon no friends, just yourself,
You will have to get used to it

When you pass, you are lonely
It's like you are in a trap
But you are really just resting
Away from the world.

Karah Smith (9)
Farrington Gurney CE Primary School, Farrington Gurney

Liverpool Vs Chelsea

The darkness of the tunnel,
The roar of the crowd,
The teams prepare for the match,
Gerrard is fired,
Lampard is very focused.

The green pitch, plain as ever,
The captains shake hands,
Liverpool have the kick-off,
Cech is now nervous,
A bad tackle by Drogba.

A free kick is awarded,
Crouch is in the box,
Cole is looking very strong,
It is now taken,
Looks like Gerrard has curled it,
And it has gone in!

Callum Davis (11)
Farrington Gurney CE Primary School, Farrington Gurney

My Thoughts

I walk down the clean, smooth carpet,
Everyone sits down feeling happy, sad and scared,
My friends and family I find,
I am lonely, lost, I feel dead.

I see the golden eagle with my beliefs,
I feel pain, loads of pain,
I am in my own world.

Bethany Ives (9)
Farrington Gurney CE Primary School, Farrington Gurney

Friends

Here comes Sally,
Walking through the valley,
Here comes Nelly,
Scratching her belly.

There's Lily,
Being silly,
Here comes Josh,
Being too posh.

Look at Maddie,
Gazing at Paddy,
Look at Peter,
Sat on the heater.

There goes Lizzie,
Who is dizzy,
Silly Fay,
Has got money to pay.

Look at Milly,
Jumping on Tilly,
Wow, look at Charles,
He's climbing the bars.

Naughty Max,
Is paying his tax,
Crazy Meg,
Is sat on an egg.

Listen to Cal,
Calling foul,
Here comes everyone,
What a lot of fun.

These are my buddies,
So you'd better run!

Paige Matthews (11)
Farrington Gurney CE Primary School, Farrington Gurney

Hate

Hate is the colour dark red and jet-black,
Hate smells like rotting fish in a frying pan,
Hate tastes like slimy mushrooms,
Hate is the number 666,
Hate is Satan in Hell,
Hate makes me feel small,
Hate cannot die, it is indestructible.

Connor Matts (10)
Monteclefe CE (VA) Junior School, Somerton

Happiness

Happiness is like a beautiful ballet butterfly
And black and white bee dancing.
Happiness is like fabulous light blue sky
And white clouds coming together gently.
Happiness is like a newborn lamb jumping in the fields
With her mummy and daddy.
Happiness is like a yellow dandelion
Sitting in the grass.
Happiness is like a little baby bear looking at the sky
Together with his brother.

Kieran Richards (9)
Monteclefe CE (VA) Junior School, Somerton

Love

The sound of love is like birds singing.
Love smells as sweet as the summer breeze.
Love is the number 3.
Love tastes like vanilla ice cream on a Sunday morning.
Love feels like a fluffy bunny.
Love looks like bees buzzing around all day.
Love is the colour of the deep blue sea.
Love is a meerkat because they always have fun.
Love is the shape of a semi-circle because it's got its ups and downs.

Alicia Harvey (10)
Monteclefe CE (VA) Junior School, Somerton

The Secrets Of Love

Love is rosy red, softly tinged with the clearest white,
Love sounds like a beautiful voice singing on Valentine's Day,
Love smells like the centre of a primrose as it travels to a
                                                    lucky person,
Love feels like a soft cloud that never breaks through,
Love is like a silent elephant grazing amongst the trees on the
                                        South African savannah,
Love would be found in the deepest part of your soul,
Love is a feeling that will never end.

Ashleigh Edwards (10)
Monteclefe CE (VA) Junior School, Somerton

Love

Love is a dark rose-red.
Love sounds like two doves singing.
Love smells like sweet-scented flowers.
Love feels like you're running through a meadow of roses.
Love is like dancing under the moon.
Love would be found by a valentine's angel.

Lucy Bond (10)
Monteclefe CE (VA) Junior School, Somerton

The Love Poem

Love is the colour creamy-white and light pink.
Love sounds like birds singing on a Sunday morning.
Love looks like the Milky Way swirling in a creamy wave.
Love tastes like a box of dark chocolates melting in front of the fire.
Love is the lucky number 1045.
If love was an animal it would be a shining, white, groomed, plaited
horse ready for the show.

Chloë Fisher (9)
Monteclefe CE (VA) Junior School, Somerton

Silence

Silence is crystal-clear
Silence sounds like nothing
Silence tastes like cool pure water running down my throat
Silence feels like flowing silk
Silence is the number zero
You'll find silence hidden in the grass, waiting for summer.

Emily Brown (11)
Monteclefe CE (VA) Junior School, Somerton

The Sweetness Of Love

Love is the colours of rose-pink and the clearest white.
Love is the sound of bluebirds singing in the morning.
Love has the taste of a chocolate with a strawberry filling.
Love smells of a tropical breeze on a Hawaiian island.
Love looks like rabbits silently hopping through the grass.
Love is like the number 3 on the 3rd of March.
Love reminds me of the happiest day of my life.
If love was an animal it would be a newborn puppy.
Love feels like a petal of a violet on your doorstep on
Valentine's Day!

Olivia Stone (10)
Monteclefe CE (VA) Junior School, Somerton

Happiness

Happiness is the colour of the bright yellow sun.
Happiness is the sound of people giggling together.
Happiness looks like a newborn baby sleeping.
Happiness tastes like honey on toast.
Happiness is my lucky number 13.
If happiness was an animal, it would be a puppy lying in the sun.

Elina Dyer (10)
Monteclefe CE (VA) Junior School, Somerton

Love

Love is the colours bright red and creamy white.
Love sounds like the strumming of violins and deep harps.
Love tastes like the sweet taste of strawberry-flavoured sweets.
Love smells like beautiful scented red roses.
Love looks like beautiful red velvet, smooth and delicate.
If love was an animal, it would be a lovely silky, shiny blue butterfly
flying in the bright blue sky.
Love would be found in your true self and in your pumping heart.
Love would be in the shape of a red, velvety, silky heart.

Cadence Lark (10)
Monteclefe CE (VA) Junior School, Somerton

Anger

Anger sounds like all the world shouting at once.
Anger is dark, evil red and demon black.
Anger tastes like mouldy, green Stilton and sour lemons.
Anger feels like sharp blades of ninja stars.

Tyler Higgs (9)
Monteclefe CE (VA) Junior School, Somerton

The Polar Bear

His nose is as cold as snow
The fur is as fluffy as a white cushion
His feet are all hard and bumpy like rocks on the beach
His teeth are as white as white paint
They roar like a lion
His tummy grumbles like a shark
He moves like a normal bear
He acts like a crocodile.

Megan Lacey (10)
Monteclefe CE (VA) Junior School, Somerton

Frost

Frost, are you there?
You never know
If the frost is there,
But,
When it does come,
It makes you glide
And slide and the
Frost can shrivel up
Leaves and can turn
Things white and
It can make icicles,
And when they melt
It's like a flowing stream
And people don't like the frost
Because it's so cold.

Emma Daley (11)
Monteclefe CE (VA) Junior School, Somerton

Love

Love is the colour of a pale pink blossom tree swaying peacefully
in the wind.
Love smells like freshly baked oven bread steaming warmly.
Love is the sound of a sparkling blue river that tinkles past the
pearly grey rocks.
Love feels like the air and the flow of happiness and light.
Love reminds me of two crossed lines joining together.
Love is the shape of a circle flowing around forever.
Love is the number 1 - the beginning.
Love is a small tabby kitten purring warmly in the sun.
Love is found beneath your soul - underneath feelings -
underneath you.

Gemma Blayney (10)
Monteclefe CE (VA) Junior School, Somerton

Anger

Anger is the colour of burning fire and jet-black.
Anger sounds like a lion roaring.
Anger tastes like mouldy chicken and dirty lemons.
Anger smells like a sour orange.
Anger looks like a big, strong thief.
Anger feels like a hot piece of ash.
If anger were an animal, it would be a phoenix.

Patrick Bromley (9)
Monteclefe CE (VA) Junior School, Somerton

Space

Billions of stars in space,
We don't go up there in case
We don't get back,
Our spaceship could crack,
But how unlikely is that?

Spaceships, stars and planets,
Meteorites and comets,
A beautiful sight,
Like a street lamp so bright,
Though the sun does help a bit.

The moon is going to bed,
As the sun is stretching his legs,
The stars stay bright,
Both day and night,
Though can only be seen when we're in bed.

Josie Mitchell (10)
Monteclefe CE (VA) Junior School, Somerton

The Sun

The moon has gone,
The sun awakes.

He shouts hooray,
A big hip-hooray.

He floats in the sky,
Like a huge, yellow balloon.

Then danger erupts,
The clouds have come,
The sun feels in danger.

A gust of wind,
The sun swishes past.

The cloud gets worried
And then he runs away.

The wind turns into a small breeze,
Although the clouds have disappeared,
The light is slowly fading.

The sun is at setting point,
Then the sun is gone,
The moon awakes.

He stretches his arms,
While the sun is asleep.

Bonnie White (10)
Monteclefe CE (VA) Junior School, Somerton

Riddles

The eyes of fire
The blazing hand
I destroy everything in my path
What am I?

The breeze of icy wind
The master of cold
I freeze everything
What am I?

The stomach of lava
The master of disaster
My stomach fluids destroy everything in my path
What am I?

Joshua Bennett (9)
Monteclefe CE (VA) Junior School, Somerton

Tornado

He stretches down from the upper world
And all is deadly still and quiet,
Until the first bolt of lightning strikes
> *Crash!*

The very first tile is stripped from the first roof
And all turns windy
People below stare with fear
At the world above
While the monster takes his place
And the skies fill with black clouds
It destroys every house, barn and shop in its path
Fierce and strong, it keeps on trudging
Trudging through the wind and rain
Filled with immaturity, it will not stop for anyone or anything.

Megan Bradley (11)
Monteclefe CE (VA) Junior School, Somerton

The Sun, Rain, Wind And Snow

The sun rises up and stretches his arms and legs.
He struggles to get into his bright yellow, summer clothes,
Like a child getting dressed.

The rain has a sound of *drip, drop, plip, plop,*
As the silver sky turns cold and grey,
The drips melt into a great silver puddle.

The wind howls as it slithers past,
It weaves in and out of objects.
You can't see the mysterious wind,
But you can hear it!

The snow is cold and white, like a polar bear,
The snow is as cold as a frozen, lemonade ice lolly.

Georgia Raybould (10)
Monteclefe CE (VA) Junior School, Somerton

Rain

The grey clouds fill the sky,
It starts to drip, drip, drip . . .
Like a tap left on.
Then suddenly the water starts to cascade down.
Umbrellas go up.

The busy crowd runs for cover.
All is quiet, the crowd comes back out,
Like a tortoise coming out of its shell.
Umbrellas go down.

The white fluffy clouds fill the sky,
Like sheep in a field.

Charlie Sillence (10)
Monteclefe CE (VA) Junior School, Somerton

The River

The river flows side to side,
It is like a giant slide.
It greets everybody that it meets.
It's so quiet you don't hear a peep,
It's so clear you can see yourself.
The water will keep you in good health,
It watches you as you pass by.
Then it looks up into the sky.
Now gone has the morning light,
So the river will rest for the night.

Rebecca Irving (10)
Monteclefe CE (VA) Junior School, Somerton

The Tornado

I spin, I spin
Like a killing monster
In the sky
I coil up like a killer snake
I destroy villages
Like a Caterpillar bulldozer.

Ryan Wheadon (10)
Monteclefe CE (VA) Junior School, Somerton

Mr Rabbit

He hops and jumps like a yo-yo.
He sniffs and snuffs like an engine.
He flops his ear like he is taking off.
His tail as fluffy as cotton wool.
His puffy body as puffy as can be.
But what he likes to do the most
Is scoff his food up like a roast.

Lauren Cattle (9)
Monteclefe CE (VA) Junior School, Somerton

The Sun

The sun rises up as the moon goes down,
The moon says goodbye,
But not with a frown.
The sun yawns and rubs his eyes,
Like he has been hypnotised.
He looks down below and all around,
There are lots of people on the ground,
But there is not a sound.
People start to go,
As the sun disappears,
The moon rises up as the sun goes down,
The sun says goodbye, but not with a frown.

Amelia Lowe (10)
Monteclefe CE (VA) Junior School, Somerton

The Horses

H orses eat green apples that shine in the sunlight,
O r long, knobbly carrots,
R un fast like a spotty cheetah chasing a deer,
S hoes like my curly, sparkly earrings,
E very day they go for a long gallop in a big field,
S addle up and away!

Sophie Waldron (8)
St Michael's Junior School, Bath

The Haunted House

H er eyes are like two balls slimed up.
A knight moves in the dark with his sword
U nder the ground is a dead man still alive
N ever, never go to the house or the garden
T oday it might be there
E very night you will hear a noise
D ead people come from under the ground and go on the street

H aunted is the house, you will remember it
O nce a man went in and didn't come back
U nder the house is a dragon with flaming fire
S ee the house at night with fear
E at the people because it's good.

Liam Herron (8)
St Michael's Junior School, Bath

Fear

F ear is very frightening
E ars point up when you are scared
A nd your heart beats fast like a cheetah
R ed is very frightening, like fear.

Trey Harding (8)
St Michael's Junior School, Bath

Doctor Who

D ark and not
O f this planet
C ould you be his companion?
T ry the door, will it open
O r is it locked?
R emember the danger that might be there

W hat could be behind?
H ow many Daleks could there be
O n the trip through time and space?

Declan Tonkinson (9)
St Michael's Junior School, Bath

The Visible Beast

Be wary of the frightful beast
As he sleepily lies in wait.
His blood is black and rotten.
His smell is like mud.
His eyes are like coal.
His nose is like a bumpy boat.
His feet are hairy and curly
And although you cannot see it,
He can see you very well!

Bradley Blackmore (8)
St Michael's Junior School, Bath

Reptiles

Geckos are big, geckos are small,
Always climbing up the wall.
Hiding all day long,
Singing their quiet song.

Snakes are short, snakes are long,
Singing their hissing song.
Slithering slowly up some trees,
Scavenging to find some buzzy bees.

Crocodiles drink and eat,
Scavenging to find some meat.
They snap their jaws
And eat lion paws.

Toby Ashman (9)
Silverhill School, Bristol

The Ghost

It feels colder than ice,
It's lighter than white,
But the room is still at its darkest.
I heard nothing,
The silence was only broken by its *howl*.
I feel sadness in its heart,
I gave it forgiveness,
But still it haunted me like a shadow,
A memory of a man or should I say *ghost*.

Louis Johnson (9)
Silverhill School, Bristol

Stupid Homework

Homework! Stupid old homework!
When I come home my mum whines at me
And says, 'Keep on the lines to me.'

She moans and groans at me to keep writing neat
But my tummy is rumbling and grumbling
Because I want something to eat.

Finished at last, homework not whizzing through my head
Time for computer games, toys and the telly
Oh no! It's time for bed.

Rosaleen Farrell (8)
Silverhill School, Bristol

My Nan

My nan is fantastic
She takes me anywhere
She picks me up on her motorbike
And fiddles with my hair

She's got a dog as soft as sheep
And a rabbit as small as a mouse
But the best thing of all is that
She has a magnificent house

I'm sure my nan is famous
I'm sure she is just that
Because when she comes to pick me up
People ask for her autograph

My nan is just so lovely
She's got very curly hair
But there is just one little problem
She wears heelys everywhere.

Anna-Louise Morgan (9)
Silverhill School, Bristol

Animal Auction

There is one rhino in the basement,
Two sleepy tortoises sleeping in my bed,
Three swans swanning around in my kitchen,
Four baby crocs on my head,
Five hyenas laughing,
Six snakes draped from my arm,
Seven mice on the piano,
Eight giraffes stuffing their faces,
Nine camels spitting on the pillows,
Meanwhile, ten forgetful foxes can't remember what they did,
So, come on, who will make the first bid?

Olivia Stewart (11)
Silverhill School, Bristol

January

January
Is a dark wet path
Cloaked in rain
Cold as snow
With *thunder* crashing down
Grey miserable clouds
Puffed-up coats
Frozen fingers
Holes in gloves
Sniffling noses
Achoo!

Jamie Stephens (10)
Silverhill School, Bristol

Cats, Cats And More Cats

Lazy little lap cat
Hiss, bite, scratch cat
Big soft-hearted cat
Climb the curtains type of cat
Little soppy-brained cat
Wander the streets cat
Big, fluffy, puffy cat
Climb the curtains type of cat
Catch mice and bird cat
Food on a plate cat
Sleep on your knee cat
Climb the curtains type of cat
Why you bothered me cat
Give me a hug cat
Whatever type of cat
It's a friend for life cat.

Chelsie Sparks (10)
Silverhill School, Bristol

January

January feels black and empty,
After the hustle and bustle of Christmas,
Sometimes lonely,
After being with lots of family for the holiday.

The burnt out grey ash - like debris of the New Year fireworks,
Beginning to rot and fade away,
No longer the roaring sparkly welcome to January,
Along with the fallen leaves, silent, wet and soggy.

Trees, naked of leaves,
Which makes a dull, stark outline on short murky afternoons,
Quickly turning into bitter inky skies of night-times.

Yet January starts to let winter go and let spring creep in,
The earth starts to share its secrets,
In the form of shoots of colour,
From the sleepy plants below.

January is the opening to the whole new year.

Katie Farrell (11)
Silverhill School, Bristol

The Rap

When you're out in the city,
Walking down the street,
A funny sort of rhythm
Starts to wiggle in your feet.

Family and friendship
Hanging over there,
All the thrill and the excitement
Floating in the air.

Kazu in the Sushi Bar
Chopping all the fish,
Putting them all into pots,
Along with two chopsticks.

Sammy playing basketball,
Slam-dunking it down through,
Almost got it, yes he did,
In basketball that's two.

When you're out in the city,
Having lots of fun,
Don't ever forget,
Who's shouting? 'Mum!'

Sam Bird (10)
Silverhill School, Bristol

Jess Has Got A Horse Called Ned

Mum, Mum, Jess has got a horse called Ned
It's got two wings, last night she went to Australia
She helped a koala stuck in a tree
She surfed with dolphins in the deep blue sea
She hopped with a kangaroo as lively as could be . . .

Mum, Mum, Jess has got a whale called Ted
It swims super fast, last night she went to Iceland
She rolled in the snow with a polar bear
She waddled with the penguins
She had tea with an Eskimo . . .

Mum, Mum, Jess has got a cheetah called Fred
It runs at the speed of light, last night she went to Africa
She roared with the lions
She swung in the trees with the monkeys
She snapped with the crocodiles . . .

Mum, Mum, I woke Jess up . . .

Ellie Seal (9)
Silverhill School, Bristol

Yellowstone

The rock at Yellowstone is as stiff as bone,
With its hissing geysers so hot
It could melt an army drone,
People think it is a cheerful place
But they will know when they're roasted like toothpaste!

Huw Tingley (9)
Silverhill School, Bristol

Cricket

Leather on willow
I dream on my pillow

Cricket in the sun
What good fun

Down the leg side
He bowls another wide

Out for a duck
That's just bad luck

Leg before wicket
It's just not cricket

Outside off stump
I give it a good thump

Rain stops play
We'll try again another day.

Harry Collins (10)
Silverhill School, Bristol

Snow

Snowball fights are just great,
They are really lots of fun,
I love it when my friends come round
And we stay out till eight.

I love to make a huge snowman
And put a carrot in his nose.
We go home and drink hot chocolate
And warm up if we can.

Toby Champion (10)
Silverhill School, Bristol

What's That Down There?

What's that down there?
What's that moving?
What's that moving down in the depths
in the murky gloom of the bottomless pit?
Is it Joker Poker?
The pink and orange kangaroo with ears that can hear a mile away?

What's that down there?
What's that moving?
What's that moving down in the depths
in the murky gloom of the bottomless pit?
Is it Pinky Minky?
The smelly, slimy cheat that crawls around in the ground
with bright glowing eyes?

What's that down there?
What's that moving?
What's that moving down in the depths
in the murky gloom of the bottomless pit?
Is it Creaker Meaker?
The impossible killer that eats you in one whole piece
and with ninety heads
in the murky gloom of the bottomless pit?

Stephanie Thorndyke (10)
Silverhill School, Bristol

The Writer Of This Poem

(Based on 'The Writer of this Poem' by Roger McGough)

The writer of this poem
Is as cracked as a cup
As daft as treacle toffee
As mucky as a pup

As troublesome as bubblegum
As hard as a brush
As difficult as a sum
As quiet as a shhh . . .

As sneaky as a witch's spell
As funky as jazz
As empty as a wishing well
As echoey as as as as . . .

As bossy as a whistle
As prickly as a pair
Of boots made out of thistles
And elephant hair

As vain as trainers
As boring as a drawer
As smelly as a drain is
Outside the bathroom door

As hungry as a wave
That feeds upon the coast
As dark as a cave
As gotcha! as a ghost

As fruitless as a cake of soap
As creeping up as smoke
The writer of this poem, I hope
Knows how to take a joke!

Emma Robinson (10)
Silverhill School, Bristol

There's A Noise In The Cave

There's a noise in the cave
It has a creepy crackling sound
The noise sounds like a giant grizzly grey bear
What is in there?

There's a noise in the cave
It is like a dark sky inside
The noise has beat
You can feel it under your feet.

There's a noise in the cave
It has a whirling, whispering wisp
The noise sounds like jumping jacks
I think there's a big loaded sack . . .

There's a noise in the cave
It has a trembling tuck sound
I can hear a howl
I think it's an owl
There's a . . .

Tvesha Parikh (9)
Silverhill School, Bristol

The Haunted Ship

'There's a ship, there's a ship,'
Let's go and explore,
Let's see if there are bones lying on the floor.

'There's a ship, there's a ship,'
Let's see what's inside,
Let's see if there are pirates hiding for their lives.

'There's a ship, there's a ship,'
I'll climb aboard, just me,
I'll see if there are pirates and parrots having their tea.

Oh no! Mum's calling us inside, must go.

Evelyn Gardner (10)
Silverhill School, Bristol

The Dream

In my dreams I dream about amazing things,
But my favourite one was . . .
The fairy dream.

I was lying on my bed,
When a fairy came to me,
It picked me up by my ears
And flew away with me.

I was scared at first
But then courage came to me,
When I looked above me to see
The bright blue fairy with butterfly wings.

I saw the galaxy,
The tiny planets,
The Earth both blue and green
And finally I saw my bare feet.

She took me high above the stars
And we even flew past the moon,
Suddenly she dropped me . . .
And I was lying back on my bed.

Ayesha Bedi (10)
Silverhill School, Bristol

The Sea - Cinquain

Crashing
Lashing, thrashing
Whirlpools raging all day
Destroying all things in the sea
Frenzy.

Joshua Tucker (10)
Silverhill School, Bristol

Red

Red is a blazing fire
Red is a ripe apple
Red is a ladybird
Red is a beautiful ruby
Red is a shining new bicycle.

Emma Portno (7)
Silverhill School, Bristol

Brown

Brown is chocolate oozing between my fingers
Brown is the old crinkly bark
Brown is the dirty mud
Brown is the rough wardrobe
Brown is a bench for friends to sit on.

Eugene Tebbenham-Small (8)
Silverhill School, Bristol

Red

Red is a blazing fire
Red is a beautiful rose
Red is a burning sun
Red is a fascinating sunset
Red is a furious bull.

Samuel Thorndyke (8)
Silverhill School, Bristol

Pink

Pink is a new baby crying
Pink is a magical flower
Pink is a pair of fluffy slippers
Pink is a squirming tongue
Pink is a bag of delicious sweets
Pink is a lovely party dress.

Emma Ujvari (8)
Silverhill School, Bristol

Yellow

Yellow is the blazing hot sun
Yellow is the beautiful buttercup
Yellow is when someone is happy
Yellow is very joyful
Yellow is a ripe banana.

Madison Dawson (7)
Silverhill School, Bristol

My Magic Boots

On my birthday, the 18th of Jan,
My mum and dad took me out in a van.
At the side of the van was a tall-looking man,
He gave me a wink and said,
'Put these magic boots on and say tut tut I think.'
He gave me a smile,
He turned around twice
And was gone by a mile.
The very next day I put the boots on,
I said, 'Tut tut,' and then I was gone
To see the world beyond.
I flew over the moon,
I soared over the ocean wide
And when I was down
I got wet by a tide.
I flew over the stars
And I finally flew over Mars
And I heard somebody shout,
'Tea is ready, come out!'

Neha Mehta (8)
Silverhill School, Bristol

Flowers

Red, yellow, pink and blue, all different kinds of flowers,
Roses, fuchsias, camelia buds which one's right for you?
I prefer the pretty pots with butterflies upon them,
Ladybirds are nice as well and flowers look pretty in them.

Izzy Tippins (7)
Silverhill School, Bristol

Colour Poem

Yellow is a ripe banana
Yellow is the blazing sun
Yellow is a delicate daffodil
Yellow is the boiling sand
Yellow is a beautiful sunflower
In the warm summer.

Sophie Walker (7)
Silverhill School, Bristol

Mammals

Some mammals are as big as a castle
Some mammals are as small as a leaf
Some are as strong as a tree
Some are as weak as grass
They are bright and dark
Some of them you can't see.

In danger they run and hide
They eat all sorts of things
Some mammals are scared of us
Some mammals don't mind
Not all mammals are friendly
Some are very kind.

Jacob Evans (8)
Silverhill School, Bristol

Snow

Snow is like a fluffy white blanket,
Snow is as cold as ice,
Snow is fun,
Snowmen and snowballing.

Scarves wrapped round necks like snakes,
Bobble hats pulled over ears,
Gloves soggy and cold,
Then the sun comes out and melts it all away.

Christian Smith (9)
Silverhill School, Bristol

The Magic Bed

One day when I was at school,
We all got called into the hall.
For someone had seen a magic bed,
With someone riding it with half a head.
And then I asked if it was my bed from home,
Sadly it said, 'Just leave me alone.'
Suddenly it whisked me off my feet,
Then brought me back to the start of the week.
But then I realised what I had done,
I forgot to say goodbye to my mum.
So then I said thank you for what it had done,
Kindly it wished I always had fun.

Lauren Childs (8)
Silverhill School, Bristol

I'm Big And Bold

I'm big and bold and as fast as a sonic boom
I glide on the water like a beautiful cruise ship
I go up high in the sky and circle my prey
I love the freedom as my feathers ripple in the wind
What do you think I am?
Why an eagle of course.

Lewis Griffiths (8)
Silverhill School, Bristol

What Is . . . Snow?

Snow is white, snow is soft, snow is cold
Snow falls down silently covering the ground like a blanket
Where fields are white with snow, children play with
                              sledges and snowballs
Snowmen stand with bright orange noses
What is . . . snow?
Snow is water, frozen into flakes
Snow is white, snow is soft, snow is cold.

Ellie-Mae Dodd (8)
Silverhill School, Bristol

Who?

'Who put the hole in the doughnut?'
'I will never know.'
'Who made Peter Pan fly?'
'Um, the wind lifted him high.'
'Who made pants so stretchy?'
'Um, I don't want to know and it's good that I don't.'
'Who made you so lazy?'
'I don't really know, I just am.'
'Who made my sister so annoying?'
'She is not annoying, OK, maybe she is a little.'
'Who made that horrible pie?'
'Um, I think that it was Nan.'
'But there is one thing I do know Dad.
    I know that you love me.'

Annalise Jones (8)
Silverhill School, Bristol

The Hunter

T eamwork is essential for success
H iding in the grass
E ventually starting to sprint

H urtling like a hurricane towards its quarry
U rgently running into a herd of scared, striped, stampeding,
spitting zebras
N imbly running through grass
T eaching the young cubs
E arly start gets goal
R avenous lions eating the kill.

Isaac Greene (8)
Silverhill School, Bristol

When I Dream

When I dream
I dream of going to tea
    with an elephant and having
        delicious buns and cakes

When I dream
    I dream of flying through a
        forest and talking to elves

When I dream
    I dream of swimming
        to the core of the Earth

When I dream
I dream of running on the sea
    and talking to whales
        on a flying surfboard

When I dream
I dream of having a better environment
    and for people to stop suffocating
        the Earth!

Daniel Randell (8)
Silverhill School, Bristol

The Crab

The crab is like a tank
They both have weapons
They both like fighting
They both are strong
They both are protected by their shell.

Julia Lawry Aguila (8)
Southville Primary School, Bristol

The Crab

The crab is like a tank,
Both are armoured,
Both need to be camouflaged,
They both have weapons,
Pinchers, guns.

Liam McDonnell (8)
Southville Primary School, Bristol

The Kangaroo

An outback long jumper,
Jumping as high as the sky,
A tail as long as a tree branch,
A bag to carry supplies.

Katie Brooks (9) & Claudia Swindale (8)
Southville Primary School, Bristol

Haiku

In the bamboo plant
At the back of my garden
My guinea pig hides.

Ellen Kendall (9)
Southville Primary School, Bristol

Worry

My life is full of worry
I'm in my own lost world
But scared at the exact same time.

My whole family in fear
Everyone in shock and despair
Waiting for an answer.

The answer is death . . . she's gone.

Phoebe Moreton (9)
Southville Primary School, Bristol

Nature - Haiku

Wind, sun and ocean
All a big part of nature
Be there forever.

Charlotte Millar (9)
Southville Primary School, Bristol

Whales - Haiku

The graceful swimmers
Drifting along the ocean
Amazing creatures.

Esmé Gottesman (10)
Southville Primary School, Bristol

Alone

Stranded on an island
in the middle of the sea
just me and nature
nobody else
I'm all alone.

Everything's peaceful
only one noise . . .
the sea.

Then I awake
away from my island
now I'm not alone.
I've got everyone
it was nice to be alone
I'm miserable now
I miss it.

Zoe Dodge (10)
Southville Primary School, Bristol

The Tortoise And Hare

Hare woke up after days,
he said, 'Oh my foolish ways.'
He jumped right up
and saw the tortoise get the cup.

'Oh my old tortoise
I've been so foolish,
I have to admit
you were right,
I was wrong!'
'Slow and steady
wins the race,'
laughed the tortoise.

Laila Elvin (10)
Southville Primary School, Bristol

The Crab

The crab is like a tank
with its hard shell
and its swift moves
They both have weapons
and they're ready for battle

They are both heavy
some bits are dark, some bits are bright
it's like camouflage.

Luther Codrington (9)
Southville Primary School, Bristol

Beachcombing

Monday I found a poem
It made me think of life
So I let it fly back to the sea
For the sea to live on.

This is how it goes:

Tuesday I found a pebble
As large as Jupiter's eye
So I skimmed it back to the sea
So the sea could read a poem.

Wednesday I found a shell full of secrets
It made me think of the secrets the world doesn't share
So I laid it back on the ocean floor
To share the sea's secrets.

Thursday I found a worn-away rock like a old man's hand
It made me feel old
So I chucked it into the sea
To make me feel young.

Friday I found a seaman's coat of tough, cracked leather
It made me think of a rowing boat rocking gently
So I let it into the sun
For the sea to dream on.

Hannah Grimes (9)
Southville Primary School, Bristol

Fun

Fun is yellow, fun is bright and makes you feel happy
and comforts you,
Fun reminds you of happiness and funny clowns
throwing custard pies.
Fun looks like a fun-filled day at an extreme theme park
with a roller coaster.
Fun sounds like a happy person screaming with joy.
Fun tastes like a huge bag of sweets.
Fun smells like my mum's home-made muffins.

Thomas Bennett (8)
The Park Primary School, Bristol

The Night

I scare cowardly children,
I am the black blanket in the sky,
I am deathly silent,
I am the night.

I am lit up by sparkling stars,
Lights are needed to see through me,
I can cause havoc on the roads,
I am the night.

I go on and on until morning comes,
Then I am gone,
I am the night.

Daniel Willey (9)
The Park Primary School, Bristol

The River

I creep through the land,
I silently flow,
I am the river.

I dash to the sea,
I tear through the world,
I am the river.

I crawl over the planets,
I leave devastation,
I am the river.

I flood quite often,
I steal your animals,
I am the river.

I tear through the rocks,
I bring worry with me,
I am the river.

I am home to fish,
I carry with me panic,
The river am I.

Ashleigh Morgan (10)
The Park Primary School, Bristol

Sternly

Sternly the headmaster bellowed at a kid,
Sternly the boy tried to open the lid,
Sternly the wave sunk the boat,
Sternly the man whipped the goat.

Sternly the dog snapped at the cat,
Sternly the bully snatched the bat,
Sternly the shout, the sternest of all,
The man piercing the little kid's ball.

Bethany Clay (9)
The Park Primary School, Bristol

Laughter

Laughter is as red as Santa's robe,
Laughter feels like telling a fabulous joke,
Laughter tastes like a great custard pie being thrown at a clown,
Laughter sounds like children playing,
Laughter smells like home-cooked birthday cake,
Laughter reminds me of a comedian,
Laughter looks like Wallace and Gromit.

James Willey (8)
The Park Primary School, Bristol

Loneliness

Loneliness feels like an empty hole in the middle of your heart,
Loneliness reminds you of your pet that has died,
Loneliness looks like a cup without its saucer,
Loneliness is black,
It sounds like a whispering mouse,
Loneliness smells like burnt chips,
Loneliness tastes like sprouts.

Katie Hollister (7)
The Park Primary School, Bristol

Laughter

Laughter is bright,
Laughter feels like you're bursting for a joke,
Laughter is happy and light,
Laughter reminds you of happy days,
Laughter tastes like a huge sun rising inside you,
Laughter feels like a huge joke in your whole body,
bouncing to every single corner.
Laughter looks like a cloud popping up,
Laughter sounds like thunder giggling across the sky.

Daniel Collins (7)
The Park Primary School, Bristol

Love

Love is the colour of love heart red,
Love feels like a new budded rose in a golden meadow,
Love smells like the flowery perfume wafting through the air,
Love sounds like the awakening birds chirping their sweet melodies,
Love tastes like a sweet strawberry, ripe from the garden,
Love reminds you of your first kiss under the lilac bush.

When love strikes you think you can float on air
like a swaying feather,
Your heart hops like a newborn rabbit.

Abbie Kidner (9)
The Park Primary School, Bristol

A Victorian Mansion Ball

Round and round the dancers go,
Side to side, to and fro.
The orchestra plays: tarrararaboom,
Tinkle, tinkle, ting ting ting, zhum.
Costumes pink, dove-white and blue,
Young faces, beautiful as the dew.
Servants hurrying down below,
Going to a place where the rich do not go.
A banquet arranged, appetisingly,
Is laid on a table from Italy.
A chandelier hangs from a golden ceiling,
A chapel upstairs where all the statues are kneeling.
A white curving staircase with a carved handrail,
A sweet snowy kitten with a fluffy tail.

Looking through the windowpane,
A small and muddy country lane.
Either side are oak trees tall,
With golden leaves that each will fall.
A neatly trimmed twisting maze,
Meets your curious young gaze.
A marble basin with crystal blue water,
Was designed by the owner's talented daughter,
Lies in the green maze's centre,
Drowned by bushes deep red-magenta!
Arriving outside the mahogany doors,
Is a splendid black carriage with velvety floors.

Out steps a woman in a silk scarlet cloak,
With a rich man, they are country folk.
They are Victoria's cousins, dressed up in finery,
They are far richer than either you or me.

Sian Collins (11)
The Park Primary School, Bristol

Storm At Sea

Clouds mysteriously growing darker and darker.
Waves getting choppier by the second.
White blurry souls storming the ship with fury.
Gigantic waves unleashing screams of terror.
Sliding feet as the ships rock with anger.
Strikes of thunder thrown from the Devil's mouth.
Choking faces struggle against the roaring ocean.

Calming weather returns,
With massive destruction around,
Frozen bodies gently drift to land.
The power of the storm.

Saleem Ali (10)
The Park Primary School, Bristol

Leaving My Friends

It is coming to the end,
Leaving my friends,
Hoping to see them soon,
Wanting to know,
Where they will go,
Having joy and fun too,
Nearly there,
Just about to go elsewhere.
Out the door,
I feel so poor,
Wanting to stay with my friends,
For evermore,
Lauren,
Lacey,
Victoria,
Frankie,
Jessica
And Jamie-Lee and Ashleigh too
And all my other friends,
I hope I will see them soon.

Shanice Loveridge (11)
Woolavington Village Primary School, Nr Bridgwater

Twenty Things Found In A Tiger's Pocket

A bag of black stripes,
Three tiny tiger cubs,
Twenty things found in a tiger's pocket.
A leg of a zebra,
Lumps of mud to build a nest for the cubs,
Twenty things found in a tiger's pocket.
A bottle of milk to feed the cubs,
Sunglasses for when it gets hot,
Twenty things found in a tiger's pocket.
Suncream so he doesn't get a tan,
A bottle of water for him to lap,
Twenty things found in tiger's pocket.
A large fan to keep him cool,
A secret present for his wife,
Twenty things found in a tiger's pocket.
Pretty blue balls,
A stone shaped like a heart.
Twenty things found in a tiger's pocket.
A pink dog's basket,
A stripy ruler,
Twenty things found in a tiger's pocket.
A watch to tell him when it's dinnertime,
A pet spider called Fred,
Twenty things found in a tiger's pocket.
A mad buffalo,
A stinky rat,
A friendly lion cub,
Twenty things found in a tiger's pocket.

Jenny Bird Davis (11)
Woolavington Village Primary School, Nr Bridgwater

Crystals

Shiny red crystals glowing as the light shines,
twinkling below the royal blue sea,
hidden inside the gloomy caves found amongst the mines.
They're found in many places,
people following their purple traces.

Matthew Moares (10)
Woolavington Village Primary School, Nr Bridgwater

Blue

Bright high sky going by,
Azure pretty bluebells puffing in the breeze,
Sapphire watery sea waving in the wind,
Turquoise colourful pen writing neatly,
Indigo leather pencil case with its stuff in it,
Navy, exciting books, people reading them,
Hard gleaming chairs sitting in the dining room.

Emma Howes (7)
Woolavington Village Primary School, Nr Bridgwater

Blue

Inky, cobalt pen in someone's hands,
Wet, soggy paint dripping off the smooth card,
Plastic tray filled with paper,
Metal, navy bottle sitting on the wooden shelf,
Sapphire cloudy sky floating around,
Fabric, bumpy lampshade hanging from the ceiling,
Flexible azure paper with writing on it,
Bendy, flat folder on a blue cabinet,
Hard china mug on the marble side,
Tired, old book in a large box.

Jake McPhee (7)
Woolavington Village Primary School, Nr Bridgwater

Green

Squishy, cuddly cushion shining in the pitch dark.
Bright jade grass used for flowers but there's not much point.
Stripy lime leaves scattered around.
Full-paged, word-filled books people use once a week.
Dry pea paper towels used for hands.
Rectangular dark boxes stuffed with books sat on the shelf.
Writable, bright card found anywhere.
Electric, working batteries all stuck in a socket.
Weak khaki pens found in a tub,.
Dark slodgy paint carried in a tub.

Jane Homewood (7)
Woolavington Village Primary School, Nr Bridgwater

Yellow

Golden hot sun in the bright sky
Wet beach sand on a hot desert
Bright, shiny gold hiding in a giant box
Hard, rough chairs sitting in old classroom
Noisy, rattly paper in a pack together
Messy running paint in a pot
Crushed, tall sunflower blowing in the strong breeze
Messy ink pens sat in a round pot.

Kayla Rossiter (7)
Woolavington Village Primary School, Nr Bridgwater

Sadness

Sadness is a blue drop of water from a tap dripping,
Sadness reminds me of miserable rainy days,
The taste of sadness is like the blue and green sea,
They look and feel like a thunderstorm from the sky,
Sadness sounds like a little girl crying,
Sadness is like a smelly seagull.

Jacob Hill (8)
Woolavington Village Primary School, Nr Bridgwater

Anger

Anger is like a boiling hot sun starting to burn,
Anger sounds like a fire cracking,
It looks like a volcano starting to explode,
It feels like rocky mountains burning,
It reminds me of burning fire,
It smells of steam coming out of a volcano,
It tastes like food burning.

Kiera O'Neill (8)
Woolavington Village Primary School, Nr Bridgwater

Fear

Fear is a black doom like the end of the world,
A fierce storm that crushes everything in its path.
It feels like a poison weakening your body,
Forcing you to turn back.
It sounds like a booming drum playing its hardest sound,
It looks like the end of the road, a black pit of doom,
                                    it's your weakness.
The smell of fear is the smell of dark smoke,
The taste torturing your tongue.
It reminds you of doom torture,
Makes you think about the end of the world,
Forces you to run to the hills.

Callum Clark (8)
Woolavington Village Primary School, Nr Bridgwater

Friends

Friends are great,
They are good mates,
Sometimes they're sad
And slightly mad.

They come in all sizes,
Full of surprises
And never let you down.

Friends are great,
They are good mates,
Sometimes they're sad
And slightly mad.

They're always there for you,
Like you are for them too.
Friends are *great,*
They are such stars,
So how many friends do you have?

Victoria Bostock (11)
Woolavington Village Primary School, Nr Bridgwater

2 Fast 2 Furious

2 Fast 2 Furious
I'm so curious,
You scratch the car, I'll get serious.

Win the race,
Turn your amps up to a bass,
Fall out your car, you'll be on your face.

Come on, use your NOS,
Time to race the fastest boss,
Win the race across the finish line,
Beat the boss in the best time.

Collect your dosh,
But I wouldn't spend it on a car wash!

Kieran Boobyer (11)
Woolavington Village Primary School, Nr Bridgwater

Horses

Trotting down the hill, the wind against my face,
Then slowing down to a quieter pace,
I get down; patting the horse,
Feeding him a carrot relished with sauce,
Giving him a mint as a very special treat,
Removing his saddle, my very comfy seat.
Treat horses with love and care,
His brown and red fur like a warm fiery flare!

Anna Lane (11)
Woolavington Village Primary School, Nr Bridgwater

Happiness

Happiness is yellow like the gleaming light of the beaming sun
rising over blooming blossoms in the summer.
Happiness tastes like the juices of a ruby-red strawberry
hanging from an emerald-green bush.
Happiness reminds me of sweet love on Valentine's Day.
Happiness sounds like a river flowing swiftly and smoothly
with birds chirping and chattering in the trees.
Happiness smells like sweet purple lavender growing big
and beautiful during the spring.
Happiness looks like a smiley face in school on a smiley face chart.
Happiness feels like the most tiny drops of rain you could ever
imagine falling softly and smoothly in your hands.

Tamsyn Stone (9)
Woolavington Village Primary School, Nr Bridgwater

Sadness

Sadness is silver droppings coming from your eyes
It smells like a bursting volcano
It feels like a burning fork in your heart
It looks like the end of the world
It tastes like rotten fish
It reminds me of Superman.

Myles O'Toole (9)
Woolavington Village Primary School, Nr Bridgwater

Happiness

Happiness is golden like the morning sun blazing.
Happiness reminds me of the moment I walk through the door
and my dog is waiting for me in the hallway.
Happiness tastes like hot bubbly cocoa on a Sunday
and smells like a ruby-red rose.
Happiness looks like the stars in the sky.
It feels like the morning dawn and sounds like someone giggling.

Keeley Sheppard (9)
Woolavington Village Primary School, Nr Bridgwater

Yellow

Bronze, glossy gold shining in a box,
Creased lemon sunflowers in the bright sun
Bright, sparkling sun shining in the sky,
Tawny soggy bananas waiting in a glass bowl,
Sandy wet sand lying on a dusty beach,
Hard plastic chairs sitting in a hot classroom,
Sharp wooden pencils in a spotty pencil case,
Shiny gleaming stars pointing in the dark sky,
Ripped amber homework books left on the slippery tables.

Beth Sparrow (8)
Woolavington Village Primary School, Nr Bridgwater

Yellow

Cream, golden sand flies in the hard breeze,
Shiny bronze sunflower growing in the hot sun,
Sandy bright sun sparkling in the high sky,
Curly school chairs with comfortable cushions,
Endless sunny drawer that has lots of paper in it,
Sparkly metal gold falling out of my pocket,
Pointed, smooth cardboard lying on the wooden table,
Bendy, sharp paper gives you bad paper cuts.

Thomas Puddy (8)
Woolavington Village Primary School, Nr Bridgwater

White

Cold crunchy snow falling from the bluey sky
Flapping clear paper on the cheery tables
Magic whiteboards with children having fun on them
Metal warm boiler on the creamy wall
Square medium plugs making electricity
Written rectangle labels stuck on cabinets
Long lit white lights lighting the giant room
Creased school T-shirts with badges on them
Ancient covered computer with people on it
Marble Coke bottle lid opening and closing
Fast spinning fan up on a squeaky cupboard.

Charly Moore (8)
Woolavington Village Primary School, Nr Bridgwater

Fear

Fear is dark like the world has ended.
It feels like rocks and ghosts are standing on you and falling.
It reminds me of when a bat came out of the attic.
It looks like a person dressed in black chasing you along
                                        a black gloomy long forest.
It sounds like someone screaming for help and creepy sounds
                                        in a bush.
It smells like mud and food with fish everywhere
It tastes of a dead frog squashed on a leaf.

Grace Ashley-Stokes (8)
Woolavington Village Primary School, Nr Bridgwater

Fear

Fear is black like a stone hand crushing the universe.
It feels like all the happiness getting drained out of you.
It smells like damp, rotten, muddy concrete covered in bats.
It tastes like burning rubber coated in slime.
It sounds like a nail scraping across thick glass.
It reminds me of somebody's body getting torn to bits
                              with a bloody knife.
It looks like a vampire getting struck by lightning
And the only thing you're thinking of is your name carved
                              on a tombstone.

Jamie Goldrich (9)
Woolavington Village Primary School, Nr Bridgwater

Happiness

Happiness is like a diamond in the rain.
Happiness smells like a circle of red roses.
Happiness looks like a joyful teacher dancing.
Happiness tastes like a cherry diamond on a tree.
Happiness reminds me of the day I met justice.
Happiness feels like a diamond in a heart.
Happiness sounds like a drum of love.

Jay Pople (9)
Woolavington Village Primary School, Nr Bridgwater

Fear

Fear is black, as black as the stormy rain clouds.
It tastes like mouldy air in your wet, soggy mouth.
It reminds me of a car crashing into a rock stone wall.
Fear smells like mud up your cold nose.
Fear sounds like someone stomping up creaky stairs.
It looks like a rock crashing down on the Earth.

Caitlin Bawdon (9)
Woolavington Village Primary School, Nr Bridgwater

Sadness

Sadness is blue like the water dripping from your eyes,
Sadness tastes like cold ice cubes,
Sadness reminds me of my hamsters,
It smells like a smelly apple,
It looks like you have no friends,
It feels like you are alone.

Callum Motion (9)
Woolavington Village Primary School, Nr Bridgwater

Happiness

Happiness is like finding a gleaming sparkling pot of gold.
Happiness tastes like a melting, special, bubbly piece of chocolate.
Happiness feels like a blazing sun building up.
Happiness reminds me of when I first saw my little sister
and when I went to my first McFly concert.
Happiness smells like bright pink flowers.
Happiness looks like a baby playing in a brand new park.
Happiness sounds like listening to McFly songs.

Chelsea Bailey (9)
Woolavington Village Primary School, Nr Bridgwater

Anger

Anger is red like a bubbling, hot, fierce volcano just waiting to burst.
Anger sounds like it is crackling, banging, bursting to explode.
Anger feels like sunburn on a hot summer's day.
Anger looks like an exploded volcano.
Anger reminds me of the wind on a windy day.
Anger smells like fire on a stick.
Anger tastes like hot food.

Chelsea Galloway (9)
Woolavington Village Primary School, Nr Bridgwater

Anger

Anger is like a red annoying world.
Anger feels like a part of you has just died
and another part of you has just been born.
Anger reminds me of my sister.
Anger tastes like the disgusting black-coloured medicine.
Anger sounds like a volcano erupting.
Anger smells like burning acid.

Jason Webster (9)
Woolavington Village Primary School, Nr Bridgwater

Anger

Anger is red-hot like a boiling hot volcano.
It feels like fire under a cooking pot.
It sounds like fire and smoke coming out of someone's ears.
It smells like sweat and fire.
It reminds me of when I got grounded.
It tastes like spicy curries.

Adam Howes (9)
Woolavington Village Primary School, Nr Bridgwater

Hammy

Hammy is my pet
And he is a very funny pet.
He climbs on his wheel
And chews all the steel.

Hammy is fluffy
But normally very scruffy.
His ears pop up
And here's what you have to say,
'I will see you tomorrow if that's OK?'
Well, that's all about Hammy,
Who is very, very funny.

Jessica Ashley-Stokes (10)
Woolavington Village Primary School, Nr Bridgwater

Fear

Fear is like the gloomy sky has gone.
The colour is dark black.
It sounds like the stormy sky shouting at me.
It feels like something chasing me across the grass.
It smells like rosy flowers in the air.
It tastes like gooey and smelly apples.
It reminds me of when I saw a ghost.
It looks like a stormy cloud.

Pia Wade (9)
Woolavington Village Primary School, Nr Bridgwater

The Soldiers At War

The soldiers shoot down planes,
The citizens are in pain,
The children get evacuated into the countryside,
The parents are at danger because their lives are at war,
Their parents are sad because they cannot see
their children anymore.

George Moore (9)
Woolavington Village Primary School, Nr Bridgwater

World War II

The soldiers shoot down planes,
The soldiers are in pain,
The parents are in danger,
But they have sandbags in the way,
I'm trying to get healthy to join the crew,
If I do I'll be happy all day.

Ross Simms (9)
Woolavington Village Primary School, Nr Bridgwater

Red

Cherry-red apples piled in a bowl,
Although I found them in a deep dark hole.
I've got a snazzy-looking pencil case,
It's one I wouldn't like to waste.
A claret jacket,
But it came in a packet.
A dark red signpost,
Which led to the coast.

Christopher Fisher (9)
Woolavington Village Primary School, Nr Bridgwater

A Knight Came Riding

A shiny knight
Came riding in the night.
The moonlight shone on the ground
The knight galloped over bridges
And he jumped over big black holes.
He galloped as fast as a cheetah.

Kieran Smith (9)
Woolavington Village Primary School, Nr Bridgwater

In A Moment Of Silence

In a moment of silence I could hear . . .
Hedgehogs rustling in the grass,
Tree leaves rustling in the wind,
Owls hooting in the trees,
Bees buzzing in the air,
Clocks tick-tocking on the wall,
Hearts beating in the distance.

In a moment of silence I could hear . . .
Birds singing in their nests,
Waves crashing on the rocks,
Rain splashing on the window,
A pencil scraping on paper.

Jack Woodman (9)
Woolavington Village Primary School, Nr Bridgwater

My Favourite Things

My favourite thing
is to ride a bike . . .
When the wind zooms through my hair
and it is as healthy as a mountain hike.

My favourite thing
is to play on the computer,
when I'm pressing the buttons
but once I've played on it too much I need an excellent tutor.

My brother's favourite thing
is to eat . . .
He thinks there's no end
and especially likes lovely juicy meat.

Sam James (9)
Woolavington Village Primary School, Nr Bridgwater

Young Writers Information

We hope you have enjoyed reading this book - and that you will continue to enjoy it in the coming years.

If you like reading and writing poetry drop us a line, or give us a call, and we'll send you a free information pack.

Alternatively if you would like to order further copies of this book or any of our other titles, then please give us a call or log onto our website at www.youngwriters.co.uk

**Young Writers Information
Remus House
Coltsfoot Drive
Peterborough
PE2 9JX**

(01733) 890066